A GRAND IDEA

HOW WILLIAM J. WILGUS CREATED GRAND CENTRAL TERMINAL

Written by **Megan Hoyt** Illustrated by **Dave Szalay**

Quill Tree Books
An Imprint of HarperCollinsPublishers

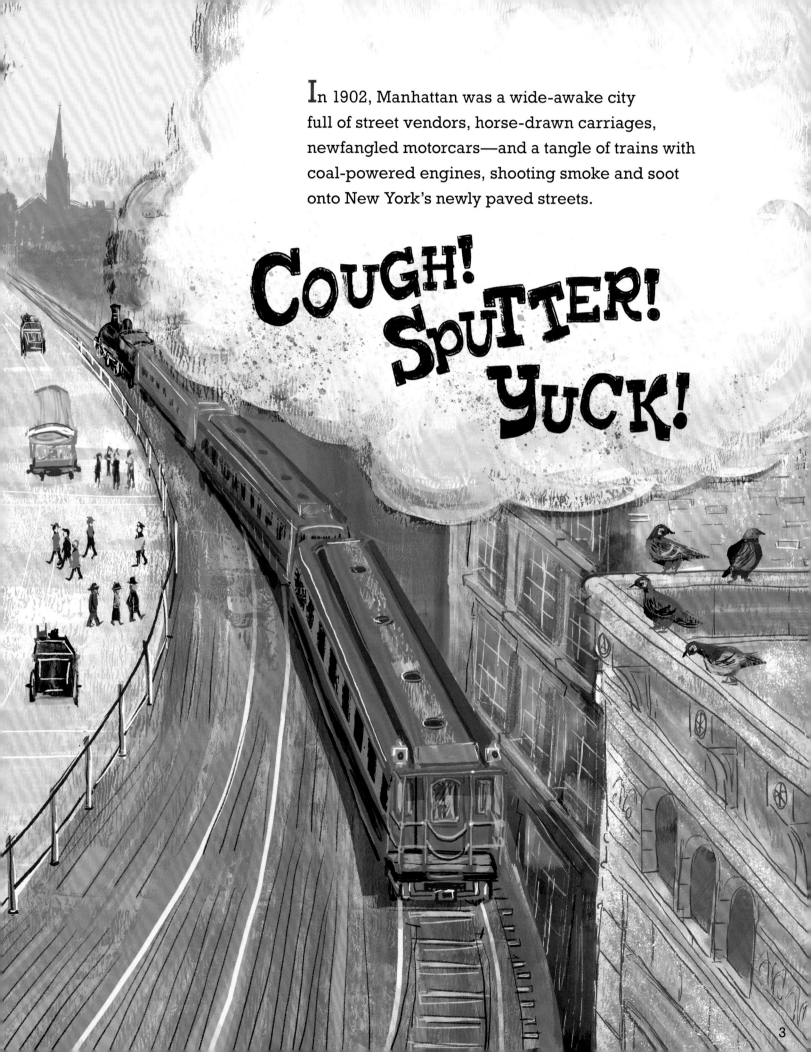

In 1902, Manhattan was a wide-awake city full of street vendors, horse-drawn carriages, newfangled motorcars—and a tangle of trains with coal-powered engines, shooting smoke and soot onto New York's newly paved streets.

COUGH! SPUTTER! YUCK!

3

Eager travelers were rushing to New York City. They came for the vaudeville shows, for the rooftop coffeehouses, for the fancy hotels and the new electric streetlights.

Some came just to be seen in the big city.

And they all arrived by train.

New York City grew and grew. Soon people from all over the world wanted to travel to the city to catch a glimpse of its glitz and glamour—and maybe spy a movie star or two. Train traffic increased even more, and before long, the traffic tangle turned into a giant snarl.

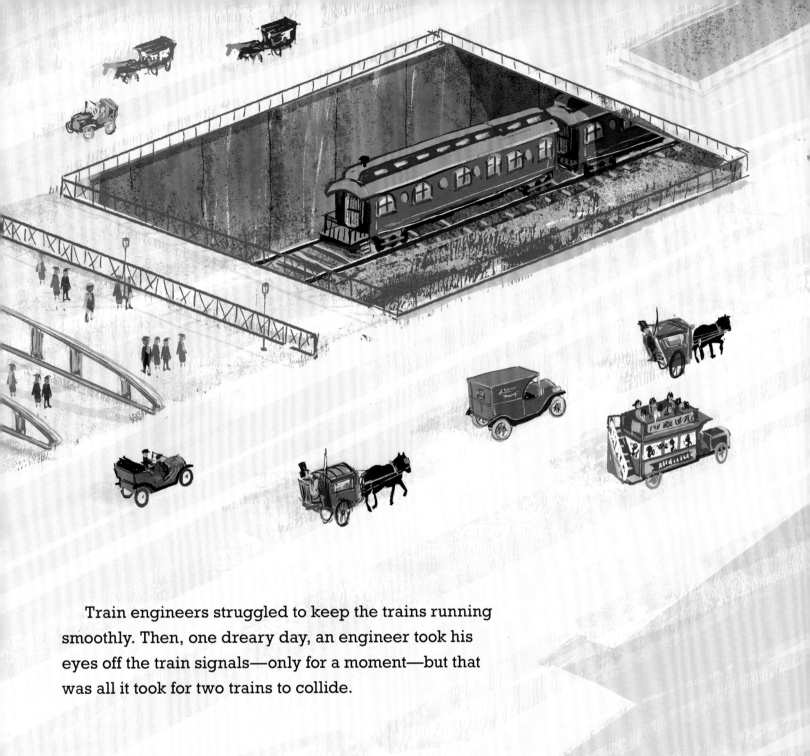

Train engineers struggled to keep the trains running smoothly. Then, one dreary day, an engineer took his eyes off the train signals—only for a moment—but that was all it took for two trains to collide.

Sparks flew.

Flames spread.

Passengers cried out in fear.

And when the coal smoke cleared, at least fifty-five people were injured, or worse.

Some blamed the train engineer. Others blamed the old, broken-down wooden cars and the dark, smoky tunnel—it was nearly impossible for an engineer to see the track ahead.

Chief engineer William J. Wilgus rushed to the scene and stared at the damaged trains. He had designed train systems in Minnesota and in Chicago. In fact, he was considered one of the best train engineers in the United States. How could this have happened right under his nose, in his new home in New York City?

More accidents were bound to happen unless he could figure out how to fix the problem.

He paced and fretted.

He focused all his concentration on the mangled mass of metal.

The smoke, the sparks, the steam . . .

An idea was brewing inside the mind of William J. Wilgus.

A great idea.

A spectacular idea.

A simply GRAND idea!

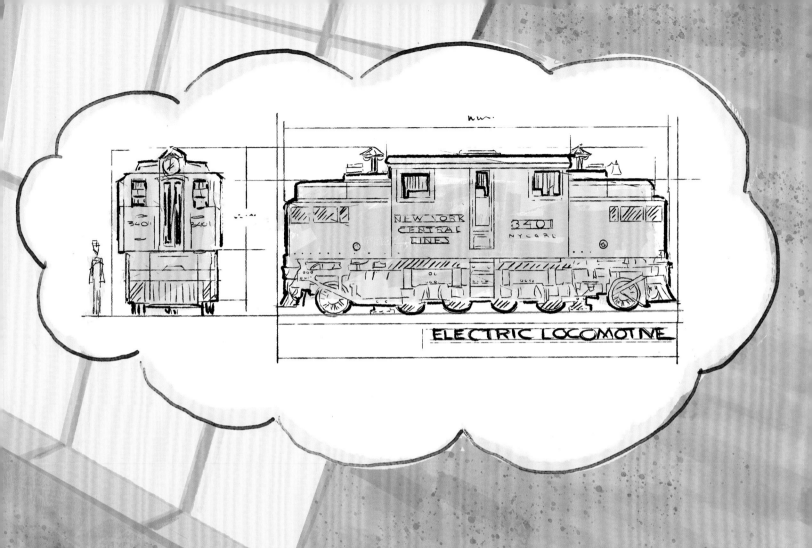

He would design a whole new fleet of steel trains to replace steam locomotives, and he'd have these trains run entirely on electricity.

No more smothering smoke.

No more soot and coal dust.

No more accidents.

Mr. Wilgus got straight to work.
He researched and measured.
He sketched and planned.
He spent long hours figuring out how to keep his new electric trains safe and secure, and he needed a third rail to do it.

To ease traffic aboveground, Mr. Wilgus came up with an even more astonishing idea. His plan would require nearly thirty thousand tons of riveted steel.

10,100 tons + 10,100 tons + 10,100 tons =
_____
30,300 tons of riveted steel

That was almost three times more metal than it took to create the Eiffel Tower in Paris, France. But he just knew it would work.

He would build two levels of train tracks *underneath* New York City.

CORNELIUS VANDERBILT

Manhattan's East Side would need a bigger train depot to house so many electric trains, and the owner of the railroad, the wealthy philanthropist William Vanderbilt, said no cost was to be spared.

"Giant oaks from little acorns grow!" was the Vanderbilt family motto, and that gave the future architects another brilliant idea. They would sneak acorns into the design of the new building as a nod to the wealthy Vanderbilt family that was financing this dream project.

It would be the biggest, grandest, most magnificent railroad station ever built. They would call it Grand Central Terminal.

Mr. Wilgus called for a contest and asked the most talented architects in America to draw up plans for the building.

Samuel Huckel Jr. designed a castle split in two by Park Avenue.

McKim, Mead & White planned a sixty-story skyscraper—the tallest one in the entire world. Above it, a three-hundred-foot illuminated jet of steam would pierce the sky, glowing red.

Reed & Stem designed a spacious Parisian-style court with enough room inside to house art galleries and an opera house.

Warren & Wetmore had designed Detroit's Michigan Central Station. It was a gorgeous building with high ceilings and large columns. They wanted to enter the competition, too, but they missed the deadline.

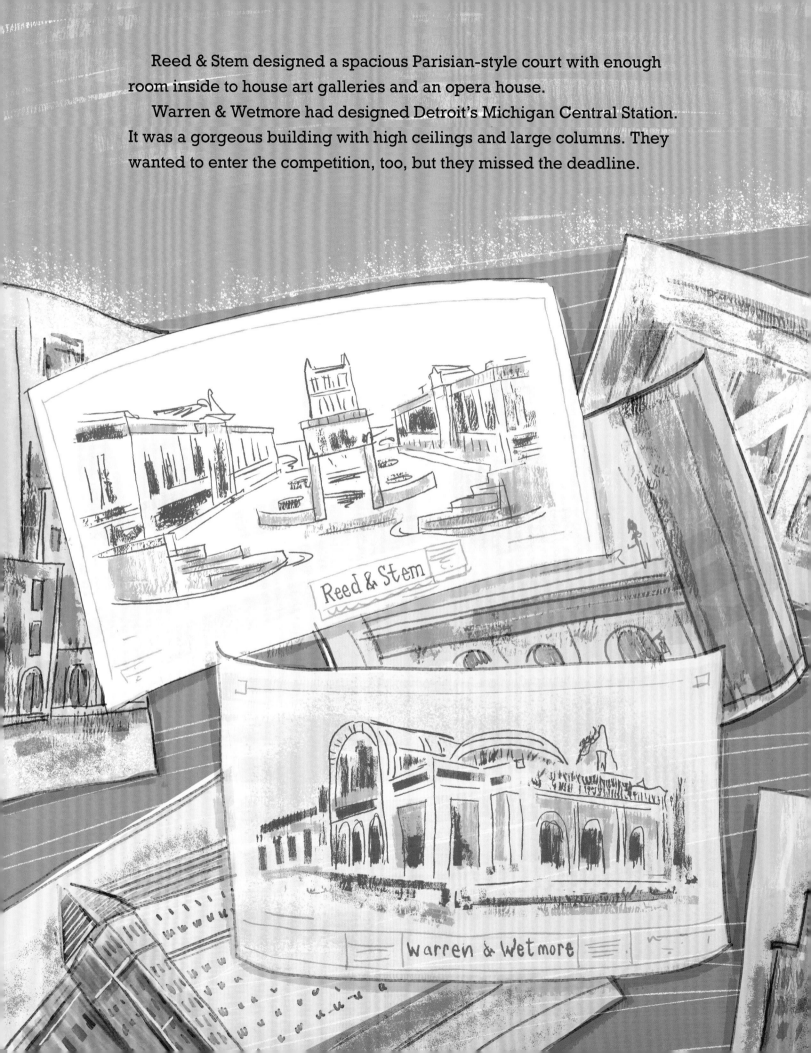

However, since Whitney Warren was William Vanderbilt's cousin, their last-minute entry was allowed.

Now it was up to Mr. Wilgus to make the final decision.

All the plans were grand, but Mr. Wilgus selected Reed & Stem's design. Since Charles Reed was his brother-in-law, this made the other architects angry. Mr. Vanderbilt wanted his cousin's firm, Warren & Wetmore. This frustrated them even more.

After tense negotiations, the two firms were forced to collaborate.

For the next eighteen months, feuding architects hashed out details. They paced. They fumed. They spent months drawing up plans and filling trash cans with crumpled paper.

Mr. Wilgus wondered if they would ever agree on a design.

Finally, they came up with a solid plan.

Grand Central Terminal's main concourse would be 275 feet long and 120 feet wide, with a ceiling towering 125 feet at its tallest point. The biggest cluster of sculptures ever built would adorn its magnificent exterior.

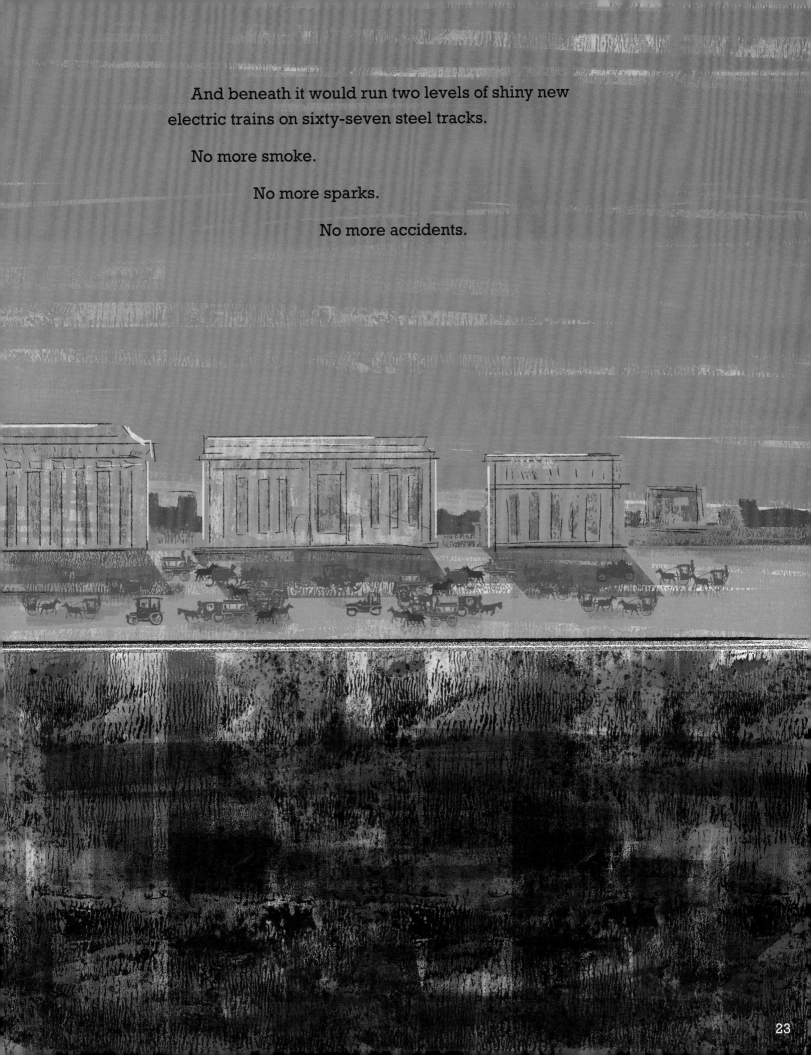

And beneath it would run two levels of shiny new
electric trains on sixty-seven steel tracks.

No more smoke.

No more sparks.

No more accidents.

Mr. Wilgus could hardly wait for the grand opening of his grand terminal. But first, railroad workers had to demolish nearly two hundred buildings and remove millions of cubic yards of rock and debris. They excavated five square blocks of land, digging thirty feet underground.

It took many years, but finally, on a brisk February day in 1913, more than one hundred and fifty thousand sightseers poured into the new Grand Central Terminal.

Its beauty overwhelmed the visitors with its sprawling bronze eagles, its giant clock, and its celestial ceiling.

It was a magical place. Building such a grand train station without computer-aided design plans, without bulldozers or modern equipment, was difficult.

Construction
workers joined sculptors,
painters, and woodworkers on
sturdy platforms built by hand. They worked
steadily, year after year. And the result was worth
every painstaking step.
When the magnificent doors opened, visitors stood, speechless, in
awe of the spectacular new terminal.

They sipped sodas and slurped oysters.
They roamed the ramps and rode the trains.
They soared up, up, up to the starry sky.

Passengers from all over the United States climbed aboard the new electric trains—hundreds, even thousands of people each day. Some were commuters heading in to work from New York State and Connecticut. Others were sightseers from faraway cities.

But railroad officials soon realized such an enormous train station costs a lot of money to maintain, and it was too expensive to run only on ticket fares.

Then William Wilgus had another grand idea.

Why not sell the air *above* the building?

"It's a gold mine," he said. "Wealth taken from the air!"

The right to own the air—it sounded silly, but if William J. Wilgus was correct, air rights could be sold for *any* New York building! If someone wanted to build a skyscraper above the underground tunnels, they would have to purchase the right to the air above Grand Central. Such a thing was unheard of, but it just might work.

Mr. Wilgus brought his idea to Mr. Vanderbilt, and soon money began pouring in.

A hospital was built at Grand Central.
A library.
A hotel.
And a movie theater.
A tennis court was built above the main concourse.
Then, the owner of the tennis court built a ski slope.
Weary travelers, energized athletes, and curious tourists flooded into Grand Central Terminal. And money flooded into Grand Central's bank accounts.

Over the years, Grand Central Terminal became a New
York City icon. Parents brought their children to the station, not
to board trains, but to tour the beautiful building.

They came for the spooky tunnels, for the rooftop view, for
the fancy restaurants, and to sneak a peek at a movie star or
two as stewards rolled out the red carpet for the most elegant
train car on the tracks—the elite Twentieth Century Limited.

Twenty years chugged past and left their mark on William J. Wilgus. He settled down on a farm in Vermont, where the puffs and whistles of locomotives gave way to the moos and clucks of cows and chickens.

Then the first passenger jet airplane took off. And almost overnight, it seemed, the glory of Grand Central chugged to a stop.

Air travel was faster and far more exciting. The railroad was on its way out. In fact, by 1975, some city planners wanted to demolish Grand Central Terminal altogether and put a giant skyscraper in its place.

But when word got out, New Yorkers were upset. This was a landmark! *Their* own grand building. They needed to save it, so they got to work. Everyday city dwellers banded together with famous New York celebrities, from uptown to downtown, led by Jackie Onassis, the widow of former president John F. Kennedy. And while railroad executives fretted and argued, Jackie took to the streets and convinced city planners to make this grand building a historic landmark.

Finally, after months of protesting and a case that went all the way to the New York State Supreme Court, the building was saved. But how would they ever draw people back to Grand Central when they could get to their destination much faster by plane?

The owners of Grand Central Terminal limped through a decade of growing debt with no answers. The building was falling into disrepair. They had to do something. Fast.

What they needed was a gigantic public event.

Something like . . .

A high-wire act!

Railroad officials called Philippe Petit, a famous French aerialist. Mr. Petit stretched a thick wire high above Grand Central's gleaming lobby. Police and train engineers hushed the crowd, and without a net, high above the gaping visitors, he stepped onto the wire.

While the audience crossed their fingers and held their breaths, step by careful step Mr. Petit walked across.

He made it!

The publicity was just what Grand Central needed. Tourists flocked to Mr. Wilgus's majestic monument—and they still do.

Now they come to find the hidden acorns.

To visit the upside-down tree.

To hunt for ghosts in the echoey tunnels.

They sip sodas and slurp oysters.

They roam the ramps and ride the rails.
They soar up, up, up to the starry sky.

And to think it all began with one man and one simply grand idea.

MORE ABOUT WILLIAM J. WILGUS AND GRAND CENTRAL TERMINAL

In 1865, the year William John Wilgus was born, bustling cities were popping up all across the United States. It was a time of great prosperity in New York City. Wealthy families showed off their elegant mansions by holding lavish parties and formal balls. Women in flowing dresses and giant hats strolled along Fifth Avenue, their heads held high.

The Vanderbilt family was among the wealthiest in the city. Cornelius "Commodore" Vanderbilt had grown his railroad empire into a gigantic train company, the New York Central Railroad. But the city grew so fast that soon their Grand Central Depot, designed by architect John B. Snook, was not big enough for the more than eleven million passengers coming to New York City by train each year. The Vanderbilts hired architect Bradford Gilbert to expand and remodel the train depot, but the renovated Grand Central Station wasn't big enough either!

And there was another problem. The railroad tracks in New York City were aboveground and cut a zipper-like line straight through the center of Manhattan. The smoke! The smog! The noise! The crowds! This was not at all what wealthy Manhattan millionaires wanted their city to look like. The Vanderbilts had already spent more than 2.5 million dollars to rebuild their train depot in 1899, but they decided to tear it down and build an even bigger one four years later.

While the Vanderbilts were building their empire in New York City, William Wilgus was growing up in Buffalo, New York. His father was a railroad foreman, and young William watched with excitement as railroads sprang up all around him. He learned everything he could about engineering, and then he left New York to take a job with the Minnesota and Northwestern Railroad in St. Paul, Minnesota. He was twenty years old with a mind full of measurements and equations and a pocket full of dreams.

In Minnesota, Mr. Wilgus created a system of underwater tunnels and developed a more efficient way to transport freight across the country. His ideas were new and far beyond what the average engineer of his day was thinking about. But his greatest achievement by far was still to come. When Mr. Wilgus was offered a job working for the New York Central Railroad, he could hardly wait to get started.

Workers began digging thirty feet down through rock and soil. Then, they had to take all the debris forty miles across town to dump it in the Hudson River. Crews demolished the area along Forty-Second Street in three phases so they could build the new terminal without any interruption to current train traffic. That included up to a hundred thousand passengers every single day. It was quite a feat!

When they heard about the design contest for Grand Central Terminal, architects from across the nation sent in their best work. Ultimately, Mr. Wilgus selected Reed & Stem, the firm whose design included a Parisian-style court. Now this was the elegant building the Vanderbilts wanted! It was in the Beaux Arts style with balconies and decorative columns, ramps, tunnels, and intricate designs sculpted in marble and bronze.

When William Vanderbilt asked the winning architects at Reed & Stem to collaborate with his cousin's firm, Warren & Wetmore, they were not happy about combining their designs. But they had no choice.

Then, at the grand opening, Mr. Warren and Mr. Wetmore took interviews with journalists, had their photographs splashed across magazines, and acted as if they were responsible for the entire design, forcing Mr. Reed and Mr. Stem and even William Wilgus into the background. Mr. Wilgus tried to correct the journalists, but he never fully received the credit he deserved for building the magnificent terminal.

Once the arguments were resolved and construction was completed, Grand Central Terminal opened right on time, at 12:01 a.m. on Sunday, February 2, 1913. It has been running ever since—closing only for a few brief power outages and railway strikes. William J. Wilgus was awarded many honors for his work and even received honorary doctorate degrees from two different universities. For a man who barely finished high school, his accomplishments, like his Grand Central Terminal, were magnificent.

FASCINATING FACTS ABOUT GRAND CENTRAL TERMINAL

TO FIND OUT MORE ABOUT GRAND CENTRAL TERMINAL, VISIT WWW.GRANDCENTRALTERMINAL.COM.

• There is a secret tunnel beneath Grand Central Terminal—track 61—where presidents arrived in the Ferdinand Magellan train car and could be taken to the Waldorf-Astoria hotel without ever setting foot inside the terminal. No one would ever know the president was arriving right below them. President Franklin Delano Roosevelt frequently traveled to New York City on track 61. He did it so no one would see that he walked with great difficulty on crutches after polio left him partially paralyzed. It is said that his dog, Fala, who often traveled with him, haunts the lower level of Grand Central. If you tour Grand Central, listen carefully. You may hear the faint whimper of a presidential Scotty dog!

• The hallway that leads to the Oyster Bar Restaurant in the lower level of Grand Central Terminal is a whispering gallery. If you stand in one corner and whisper something, a friend will hear it across the room in the opposite corner.

• The movie theater opened in 1937 with a lounge designed by Tony Sarg, who also designed the first Macy's Thanksgiving Day Parade balloons.

• The ski slope at Grand Central was not made of real snow but a material similar to toothbrush bristles.

• There is a glass walkway between the windows of Grand Central Station. So don't be alarmed if you see someone "walking on air" like a ghost.

• Ever heard of rolling out the red carpet? That phrase came from the elegant express train, the Twentieth Century Limited. Whenever it arrived at Grand Central from Chicago filled with movie stars and celebrities, a red carpet was always unfurled so the elegant ladies and gentlemen wouldn't muss their shoes on the dusty platform as they stepped off the train.

• There is a library inside Grand Central Terminal that houses more than three thousand books, photos, and newspapers along with a section of the red carpet from the Twentieth Century Limited.

• "Great oaks from little acorns grow" was the Vanderbilt family motto. If you look carefully, you will find acorns and oak trees as design elements throughout Grand Central Terminal.

• Until 1963, there was a hospital inside Grand Central Terminal. It began as a temporary center to treat railroad workers in case they were injured on the job, and in 1911 the Grand Central Emergency Hospital opened its doors. There was even an operating room!

• If you look closely at the chandeliers, you'll notice that all the light bulbs are on the outside exposed. That was done to show off the fact that Grand Central Terminal had electric lighting. Most homes and businesses still used oil lamps and candlelight.

A GRAND TIMELINE

Terminal Design, Construction, and Inventions around the World

1871   New York Central Railroad's Grand Central Depot opens on October 7.

1899   William J. Wilgus is made chief engineer of the New York Central Railroad. He suggests electrifying the entire railway line in New York City. His plan is deemed too expensive and is not approved.

1900   A new century begins!
The Grand Central Depot reopens as Grand Central Station. The new station cost $2.5 million to build, but it was soon torn down to build the giant new Grand Central Terminal.
The world's first Zeppelin takes flight in Germany on July 2.
The portable Brownie camera is invented by the Eastman Kodak company.

1902   A train collides with another in the Park Avenue Tunnel in New York City on January 8.
The elegant Twentieth Century Limited train is launched and runs until 1967, taking celebrities and dignitaries to their destinations.
The air conditioner is invented.
The first movie theater opens in Los Angeles, California, on April 16.

1903   William J. Wilgus is appointed vice president in charge of construction at the New York Central Railroad.
Architects compete to design Grand Central Terminal.
The Wright brothers' first recorded flight occurs on December 13.
Windshield wipers are invented.

1904   Warren & Wetmore and Reed & Stem codesign Grand Central Terminal in the Beaux Arts style.

1905–06   Seventy acres of apartments, office buildings, and factories are cleared, and 3.2 million cubic yards (ten floors deep) are excavated in preparation for the two-level, sixty-seven track underground train system at Grand Central Terminal.

1908–13   Construction of Grand Central Terminal continues—thirty-two miles of track and thirty platforms took nearly thirty thousand tons of steel to build.

1909   William J. Wilgus is awarded the Thomas Fitch Rowland Prize for his work on bringing electric rails to New York City.

1913   Grand Central Terminal officially opens at 12:01 a.m. on Sunday, February 2.
A barbershop, a laundry service, and a shoe store also open at Grand Central Terminal.

1918   Giant American flags are hung in Grand Central Terminal to honor the men fighting in World War I.

1919   The Commodore Hotel beside Grand Central Terminal opens on January 28.

1921   William J. Wilgus is granted an honorary doctorate degree from the Stevens Institute of Technology.

1923   The Grand Central School of Art opens on the seventh floor, along with the Grand Central Art Galleries.

1926	Land around Grand Central Terminal more than triples in value since 1904.
1927	William J. Wilgus is granted an honorary doctorate degree from the University of Vermont.
1928	Mary Read begins playing organ music inside Grand Central Terminal at Christmas to cheer up weary passengers. Travelers enjoy it so much that the railroad hires her to perform at the terminal until she retired in the late 1950s.
1930	Construction begins on the Waldorf-Astoria hotel near Grand Central Terminal. William J. Wilgus officially retires and moves to Vermont.
1938	Track 61 is used as a secret passage from Grand Central Terminal to the Waldorf-Astoria hotel.
1941	A large mural is created and hung in Grand Central Terminal to encourage passengers to buy war bonds to help fund World War II.
1942	William J. Wilgus receives the Wellington Prize for outstanding contributions in engineering.
1949	William J. Wilgus dies peacefully after a brief illness on October 24, at the age of eighty-three.
1954	Passengers begin driving or flying to their destinations, leading to a decline in train ticket sales. An architectural firm proposes that Grand Central Terminal be torn down and replaced by a skyscraper with shops and a rooftop helicopter landing pad.
1966	The Vanderbilt Tennis Club opens.
1967	Grand Central Terminal is designated a New York City Landmark.
1969	The first US astronauts land on the moon on July 20.
1971	Ticket windows at Grand Central Terminal are used for placing bets on horse racing. The first commercial video arcade game is developed.
1974	The first personal computer is developed.
1975	In a speech to help save Grand Central Terminal after further attempts at restructuring, Jacqueline Kennedy Onassis says, "Americans care about their past, but for short-term gain they ignore it and tear down everything that matters. Maybe . . . this is the time to take a stand, to reverse the tide, so that we won't all end up in a uniform world of steel and glass boxes."
1976	Grand Central Terminal is declared a national historic landmark.
1987	Philippe Petit walks a high wire eighty feet above a hushed crowd at Grand Central Terminal.
1988	Grand Central Terminal's seventy-fifth anniversary
1995–98	Grand Central Terminal is revitalized. The vast ceiling is cleaned, and the Grand Central Market opens. Today, Grand Central Terminal houses more than sixty shops, thirty-five restaurants, a market, tennis club, Transit Museum, whispering gallery, oyster bar, secret tunnels, and holiday fairs.

SOURCES

"A Look Back at Grand Central Terminal Through the Years." *Daily News*, February 1, 2018. www.nydailynews.com/new-york/grand-central-terminal-turns-100-gallery-1.1251094?pmSlide=1.1251085.

Agins, Tamara. "The Top 10 Secrets of NYC's Grand Central Terminal." *Untapped New York*. www.untappedcities.com/2017/12/13/top-10-secrets-of-grand-central-terminal.

Ahmed, Beenish. "A Grand Central Ghost Story." WYNC News, October 31, 2017. www.wnyc.org/story/grand-central-ghost-story.

Attwooll, Jolyon. "Grand Central Centenary: 100 Fascinating Facts." *Telegraph*, January 31, 2013. www.telegraph.co.uk/travel/destinations/north-america/united-states/articles/Grand-Central-centenary-100-fascinating-facts.

Black, Annetta. "Uncovering Grand Central Terminal's Secret Spaces." *Atlas Obscura*, January 31, 2012. www.atlasobscura.com/articles/uncovering-secrets-of-grand-central-terminal-new-york-city.

———. "Grand Central Terminal Whispering Gallery." *Atlas Obscura*, December 12, 2012. www.atlasobscura.com/places/grand-central-terminal-whispering-gallery.

Carlon, Jen. "Did You Know That There Used to Be a Movie Theater in Grand Central Terminal?" *Gothamist*, April 22, 2015, modified August 20, 2018. www.gothamist.com/arts-entertainment/did-you-know-there-used-to-be-a-movie-theater-in-grand-central-terminal.

Casetext. *Stem v. Warren*. January 13, 1920. www.casetext.com/case/stem-v-warren-4.

Dorfman, Dan. "Fault." *New York Magazine*, October 27, 1975. www.books.google.com/books?id=ZugCAAAAMBAJ&printsec=frontcover&source=gbs_ge_summary_r&cad=0#v=onepage&q=fault&f=false.

Epstein, Michael, dir. *American Experience*. Season 20, episode 4, "Grand Central." Aired February 4, 2008, on PBS. www.pbs.org/wgbh/americanexperience/films/grandcentral.

Fermino, Jennifer. "'Grand' Entrance—Famed WTC Daredevil Philippe Petit on Track for Station Feat." September 11th Families' Association, April 2, 2012. www.911families.org/grand-entrance-famed-wtc-daredevil-on-track-for-station-feat.

"Fifteen Killed in Rear End Collision: Trains Crash in Darkness of Park Avenue Tunnel." *New York Times*, January 9, 1902. www.nytimes.com/1902/01/09/archives/fifteen-killed-in-rear-end-collision-trains-crash-in-darkness-of.html.

Gannon, Devin. "FDR's Beloved Dog Is Said to Haunt Grand Central Terminal's Secret Train Track." *6sqft*, October 31, 2017. www.6sqft.com/fdrs-beloved-dog-is-said-to-haunt-grand-central-terminals-secret-train-track.

Grand Central Terminal. "Contact: How Can We Help You?" www.grandcentralterminal.com/contact.

Grundhauser, Eric. "Vanderbilt Tennis Club." *Atlas Obscura*, October 3, 2014. www.atlasobscura.com/places/vanderbilt-tennis-club.

Moore, Derry. "Presidential Passage: A National Landmark, the Private Railcar Ferdinand Magellan Served Four U.S. Leaders." *Architectural Digest*, September 30, 2008. www.architecturaldigest.com/gallery/railcar-slideshow.

Moser, Emily. "A Visit to the Secret Library Inside Grand Central Terminal." Ride the Harlem Line, November 30, 2012. www.iridetheharlemline.com/2012/11/30/a-visit-to-the-secret-library-inside-grand-central-terminal.

———. "The Electrification of Grand Central, and Metro-North's Third Rail." Ride the Harlem Line, February 13, 2015. www.iridetheharlemline.com/2015/02/13/the-electrification-of-grand-central-and-metro-norths-third-rail.

New York Transit Museum. "Grand by Design: A Centennial Celebration of Grand Central Terminal," 2014. www.gcthistory.com/#intro.

Railway Review, July–December, 1915. Vol. 57. Chicago, 1915. play.google.com/books/reader?id=jAVCAQAAIAAJ&hl=en&pg=GBS.PP6.

Roberts, Sam. "100 Years of Grandeur." *New York Times*, January 18, 2013. www.nytimes.com/2013/01/20/nyregion/the-birth-of-grand-central-terminal-100-years-later.html.

Schlichting, Kurt C. *Grand Central Terminal: Railroads, Engineering, and Architecture in New York*. Baltimore: Johns Hopkins University Press, 2001.

———. *Grand Central's Engineer: William J. Wilgus and the Planning of Modern Manhattan*. Baltimore: Johns Hopkins University Press, 2012.

Tell, Alex. "Money's in the Air." *Avery Review*. www.averyreview.com/issues/39/moneys-in-the-air.

Waldman, Benjamin. "The New York City That Never Was: Grand Central Terminal." *Untapped New York*. www.untappedcities.com/2013/02/01/the-new-york-city-that-never-was-part-vii-grand-central-terminal.

Weingart, Richard G. "William J. Wilgus and Grand Central Terminal." ASCE Library. www.ascelibrary.org/doi/10.1061/%28ASCE%29LM.1943-5630.0000094.

Whitmore, Geoff. "Changes Coming to the Grand Hyatt New York." *Forbes*, February 21, 2019. www.forbes.com/sites/geoffwhitmore/2019/02/21/grand-hyatt-new-york-to-be-torn-down/#932ea6976155.

Wind, Herbert Warren, Rosann Smith, and Brendan Gill. "Heartaches." *New Yorker*, December 19, 1947. www.newyorker.com/magazine/1947/12/27/heartaches.

For Anthony, Levi, Emmett, and Balthazar
—M.H.

For Christy Ewers—the journey really began at Grand Central Terminal!
—D.S.

Quill Tree Books is an imprint of HarperCollins Publishers.

A Grand Idea: How William J. Wilgus Created Grand Central Terminal
Text copyright © 2024 by Megan Hoyt. Illustrations copyright © 2024 by Dave Szalay. All rights reserved.
Manufactured in Italy. No part of this book may be used or reproduced in any manner whatsoever without written
permission except in the case of brief quotations embodied in critical articles and reviews. For information address
HarperCollins Children's Books, a division of HarperCollins Publishers, 195 Broadway, New York, NY 10007.
www.harpercollinschildrens.com

Library of Congress Control Number: 2022930102
ISBN 978-06-306474-4

The artist used Adobe Photoshop to create the digital illustrations for this book.   Typography by Rachel Zegar

23 24 25 26 27 RTLO 10 9 8 7 6 5 4 3 2 1   First Edition